THIRD EDITION
DISCOVER YOUR GIFTS

AND LEARN HOW TO USE THEM

ALVIN J. VANDER GRIEND

LEADER'S GUIDE

FAITH
ALIVE®
Christian Resources

Grand Rapids, Michigan

We are grateful to Alvin J. Vander Griend for his contributions in planning and revising this third edition of *Discover Your Gifts and Learn How to Use Them* (revised and expanded from *Discover Your Gifts*, first published by Christian Reformed Home Missions in 1980 and updated in 1983, then revised by Faith Alive in 1996).

We also acknowledge with gratitude the gifts of the following persons who contributed to earlier editions: advisors to the original *Discover Your Gifts* were Cliff Christians, David Holwerda, Norman Meyer, and Marion Snapper. Wesley Smedes and Dirk Hart made significant contributions as members of CRC Home Missions staff. Henry De Rooy was project coordinator. Consultants for the 1983 update were Del Nykamp and Mike McGervey, and Edi Bajema provided editorial assistance. David Armstrong, Carl Bosma, Phil Noordmans, Jackie Timmer, Henry Wildeboer, and Randal Young served as advisors for the 1996 edition. Don McCrory served as editor for that edition, and Duncan McIntosh provided input as a denominational leader and spiritual-gifts trainer. Appreciation is due also to thirty pastors and churches who field-tested the material prior to publication of the 1996 edition.

In presenting this 2008 edition, we thank Neil Carlson of the Center for Social Research at Calvin College for assessing the Discover Your Gifts Survey, and we thank Bob Rozema, former curriculum editor at Faith Alive, for pedagogical counsel on revising lessons and other elements. In addition, we thank numerous church leaders, course participants, and other consultants whose responses to surveys and evaluations helped shape this third edition.

Unless otherwise indicated, the Scripture quotations in this publication are from the Holy Bible, Today's New International Version™ (TNIV). © 2001, 2005, International Bible Society. All rights reserved worldwide.

We welcome your comments. Call us at 1-800-333-8300 or e-mail us at editors@faithaliveresources.org.

ISBN 978-1-59255-408-9

5 4 3 2 1

CONTENTS

LETTER TO CHURCH LEADERS

Dear pastors and other leaders:

Is the following statement too close to the truth in your church: "20 percent of our people are doing 80 percent of the work"? Hopefully your church is doing a lot better than that, but perhaps you still wish a greater percentage of your members could be involved in meaningful ministry. You and others may be busier than you should be, while many of your members may be sitting on the sidelines.

As you know, that isn't the way Christ wants the church to be. The New Testament presents the church as a body of believers equipped and empowered by the Holy Spirit, mobilized for ministry. Many leaders have to remind people regularly that church is not an event to attend. It's a group of people ready to build the kingdom of Christ and to bring the gospel to the ends of the earth.

How can we recover Christ's vision for the church? A first step is to help people know who they are in Christ and that they are called to service in God's kingdom. A second step is to help people discover their gifts and learn how to use them. A third step is to help people identify the specific ministries for which Christ has gifted them and to bravely step into those ministries.

That's what *Discover Your Gifts and Learn How to Use Them* is all about. It's a practical course of study designed to help you lead your church members to discover their spiritual gifts and put them to use in ministry. The end result will be not only increased knowledge but also more servants of Christ actively engaged in ministries that help build the kingdom of God.

For his glory,

Alvin J. Vander Griend

INTRODUCTION

INTRODUCTION

About the Course

This leader's guide is meant to accompany the student book of *Discover Your Gifts and Learn How to Use Them*. It includes a complete set of teaching notes for the course instructor, follow-up suggestions on forming a Gift Leadership Team, various options for using the course, and sermon notes for pastors who would like to preach a sermon series on spiritual gifts.

The sessions should take about 60 minutes (see suggested time-frames for each lesson segment). In some cases you may need more time, depending on the makeup of your student group. However, you may certainly adapt the lesson material to fit the available time you have.

Optional Ways to Use *Discover Your Gifts*

In addition to the five-session format presented in this guide, this course can be used profitably in the following formats (for more information on these, see Appendix B):

- three-session *Discover Your Gifts* course
- two-session course
- one-session class (perhaps as part of a new members class)
- one-day intensive workshop
- overnight retreat workshops
- whole-church *Discover Your Gifts* emphasis

Follow-up Procedures

Discover Your Gifts and Learn How to Use Them may be used effectively as a course for those who simply want to study spiritual gifts. But the full value of this course will be missed if its use stops there. It's very important to implement follow-up procedures so that people will move from study into ministry. Ministry, not academic learning, is the ultimate goal of this course. To accomplish this goal, most churches will need to repeat this course several times until a majority of members have discovered their spiritual gifts and are using them in ministry.

To make sure that ministry *is* the end result, someone—the church's pastor(s), administrator(s), executive team, or an *ad hoc* group of ministry leaders—needs to embrace the vision for a church engaged in gift-oriented ministry, identify ministry opportunities, oversee the ministry-placement process, facilitate the development of new ministries to which God is calling the church, and encourage support systems for those in ministry. Some churches may want to place the challenge of managing this process in the hands of a Gift Leadership Team (see Appendix A).

Engaging the church in a spiritual-gifts approach to ministry is a worthy, God-glorifying objective. From the beginning God intended the church to be not simply a group of Christians who gather to celebrate in worship but fundamentally a ministering body.

Preparing for the *Discover Your Gifts* Course

Church leaders who are responsible for the church's ministries should prepare for this course as follows:

1. Assess the congregation's need for discovery, development, and deployment of spiritual gifts. Ask questions like these: What percentage of the congregation is now involved in ministry? How will church structures be affected? What current practices and attitudes will be challenged? What will be gained?

2. Identify and describe the church's ministry positions to be filled by those who have discovered their gifts. Begin thinking about new ministries where none now exist in order to provide ministry opportunities for members who are discovering spiritual gifts.

3. Analyze the church's organizational structures and make sure that they facilitate gift-based ministry. Recommend necessary changes.

4. Promote the gift-discovery course to the congregation and help to recruit class members.

5. Prayerfully select instructors for the course and give them whatever support they need.

6. Provide opportunities for members who have discovered their spiritual gifts to receive training that will help them develop their gifts further in ministry.

7. Plan for and keep records of spiritually gifted members and the ministries in which they serve and are needed.

8. Help place members who have identified gifts into ministry positions, inside or outside the church, where they can be fruitful.

Discover Your Gifts Teachers

Teachers should

- have the spiritual gift of teaching.

- understand and own the gift vision of the church.

- be able to facilitate learning in a participative style.

- read through the entire gift course before the first session.

- prepare their hearts by acknowledging God's call on their lives, recognizing their own limitations, and seeking through prayer the grace and strength to be effective in this ministry.

Teachers are

- instructors able to clarify the concepts being taught and to reinforce the value of the course.

- facilitators able to direct and oversee small group learning activities.

- encouragers able to support and help empower church members who may be timid about their God-given ability to engage in ministry.

- intercessors who plead for the infusion of God's power and grace into the lives of class members.

Discover Your Gifts Teaching Methods

- **Small groups.** Small groups are an important part of this course. Every session provides for small group time, offering a comfortable way for everyone to participate. The smaller the group (no more than three or four persons), the more talk time each person has. Don't let your small groups get too large. Try to meet in a space that will facilitate a comfortable small group arrangement.

- **Bible discovery.** Every class session includes valuable Bible study time. The Bible passages to be studied are printed in the student book. The discovery questions in the sessions can be answered from these printed passages. However, you may want to urge class members to bring and use their own Bibles so that they can work with these passages in their scriptural contexts.

- **Teaching segments.** Every class session also includes teaching segments in which you, as leader, will be expected to present content. The content is usually supplied in Part B: FAQs About Spiritual Gifts in the student book, allowing you the freedom to summarize, expand on, or highlight what is presented there. As your students read from these sections after the class sessions, what you have taught will be reinforced.

- **Prayer times.** Opening and closing prayer times are important. Try to tie these into the subject matter of each class session. Engage class members as often and as fully as possible in these prayer times. Be careful, though, not to force people into praying out loud or in small groups if they are uncomfortable doing so. Note the suggestions for prayer times that are given in this leader's guide, but feel free to alter those to fit your group.

Discover Your Gifts Participants

Course participants should understand that they will be expected to

- attend all the class sessions unless a major conflict is unavoidable.

- complete homework assignments between class sessions.

- participate in small group sharing and activities.

LEADER'S NOTES FOR SESSIONS

WHAT THE BIBLE SAYS ABOUT SPIRITUAL GIFTS

Opening Prayer (1 minute)

In this first session the leader should offer the opening prayer.

Preview (1 minute)

After seeing that each person has a student book, invite everyone to open to session 1 and look over the Preview at the beginning of the session notes. Read this section with the group to explain what you're going to cover together in this first session.

Warm-up Exercise (3-5 minutes)

Quickly divide your group members into small groups of three or four. To start things off, invite people to introduce themselves within their small groups and tell one or two things about themselves. Have them also tell about one of the best gifts (of any kind) they ever received. Give each person about a minute so that everyone has a time to speak.

> *Tip:* If you think you'll need an extra five or so minutes for this Warm-up Exercise, you can spend less time on the Bible Discovery step and ask people to complete unfinished parts of that step at home.

Bible Discovery (25 minutes)

Continue in the same small groups for this Bible Discovery exercise. Encourage everyone to work together in their small groups by reading the Scripture passages in their student books and answering the discovery questions after each passage. Alert groups to the 25-minute time frame and tell them that when they are finished, the whole class will work to pull their thoughts together by answering some *who, what, where, why,* and *how* questions. If people get stuck on any questions, let them know they will probably get answers in the next part of the session.

> *Option:* Divide up the Scripture passages among the small groups so that each group gets one longer passage and a couple of shorter ones.

Pulling Our Thoughts Together
(10-12 minutes)

Call everyone back together and lead a whole-class question-and-answer time in which people share what they have learned during their Bible study exercise. Ask the *who, what, where, why,* and *how* questions about spiritual gifts. Invite answers from everyone. Encourage people to make note of the answers given. Suggested answers with references are printed below, along with some additional insights.

Spiritual Gifts

- **What are spiritual gifts?** Spiritual gifts are grace-given abilities. The Greek word for gifts usually translated as "spiritual gifts" is *charisma*. It comes from the Greek word *charis,* which means "grace." The word *charisma* occurs seventeen times in the New Testament. It literally means "grace gifts." Spiritual gifts are abilities given to individual believers in the community of Christ—Rom. 12:6; 1 Cor. 12:4; 1 Pet. 4:10. (This question is covered in more detail in the next section: Unpacking a Definition.)

- **Who gives these gifts?** Spiritual gifts from God are given by Christ through the Holy Spirit—1 Cor. 12:4-11; Eph. 4:11.

- **To whom are they given?** Spiritual gifts are given to every believer in the body of Christ—Rom. 12:6; 1 Cor. 12:7; 1 Pet. 4:10.

- **Why are they given?** Spiritual gifts are to be used for the benefit of others. They are abilities that enable believers to minister effectively to others. God uses spiritually gifted individuals to enrich the lives of fellow brothers and sisters in the body of Christ, to the glory of God—1 Cor. 12:7; Eph. 4:12-13; 1 Pet. 4:10-11. See also question 3 of FAQs About Spiritual Gifts (Part B) in the student book.

- **Where do they function?** Spiritual gifts function chiefly within the church. The church, which is the living body of Christ, is an interdependent community in which members belong to one another and serve one another with their Spirit-given abilities—Rom. 12:4-8; 1 Cor. 12:7, 12-27.

- **How do they function?** Gifts must function in the context of love. They are worth nothing unless exercised out of love. The community in which they function is meant to be a community marked by love—1 Cor. 13:1-3; 1 Pet. 4:8.

Unpacking a Definition (7-10 minutes)

The definition below is amplified further in question 2 of FAQs About Spiritual Gifts (Part B) in the student book. Use that material to develop your own brief presentation on the definition of spiritual gifts. Speak briefly about each part of the definition. Group members should be ready to absorb this content after the two segments they have just completed.

> **Spiritual gifts are special abilities given by Christ through the Holy Spirit to empower believers for the ministries of the body.**

- special abilities—

- given by Christ—

- through the Holy Spirit—

- to empower believers—

- for the ministries of the body—

When you have finished your presentation on the definition, give everyone an opportunity to ask questions or add comments. Some issues that may come up for further discussion:

- **special abilities**—"special" here means out of the ordinary, beyond what is normal. An "ability" could also be called a strength, an enablement, an empowerment, an endowment, or a competency.

- **given by Christ**—God the Father is also involved (see "Who gives these gifts?" above). The roles of the Father, Son, and Holy Spirit are often understood in terms of the Father's planning and initiating, the Son's working out of the Father's will, and the Holy Spirit's delivering to the end user (us) what the Father has planned and the Son has worked out. These are essentially the roles of the Father, Son, and Spirit in giving us spiritual gifts.

- **through the Holy Spirit**—It may help to reinforce that the Holy Spirit, as the third person of the Trinity, is truly a thinking, feeling, willing, acting, communicating, listening person who never operates independently but always carries out what the Father wills and what the Son has made possible.

- **to empower believers**—nonbelievers have God-given abilities too. God provides all the abilities, strengths, talents, and skills that humans have. However, the Bible doesn't call the abilities of nonbelievers spiritual gifts—probably because they are not used for the work of ministry, the building up of the church and kingdom, or the glory of God.

- **for the ministries of the body**—the word *ministry* is often used interchangeably with the more common word *service*. We are not talking here about the work of the preacher who is sometimes called "the minister" but about all ministries of the members of the church of Christ. Though ministries are primarily for and within the body of Christ, they also operate outside the church to advance the kingdom of God.

Looking Ahead (1-2 minutes)

Before you close this session, underscore the importance of assignments to complete before the next session. You may want to note the Guidelines for Participants in the front material of the student book to remind everyone of general expectations for class participation. One of the best encouragements you can give is your own testimony of the value of "after session" assignments and follow-up study. Invite everyone to turn to Part B: FAQs About Spiritual Gifts and Part C: Gift Studies in their books to note follow-up reading and study that they can do to their benefit.

Closing (3-4 minutes)

If class members are reasonably comfortable praying with others in small groups, have them gather into their earlier small groups to end this session in prayer. Point out the three prayer suggestions at the end of the session in the student book. Note that people can easily expand on the *praise, thank,* and *ask* ideas referenced there. Acknowledge that some group members may wish to be silent "pray-ers."

If many of the class members are not comfortable praying by themselves in a small group, offer a closing prayer yourself. Introduce the prayer with a reminder that you will pick up on the three elements that are referenced in the closing suggestions: *praise, thanks,* and *asking.*

DISCOVERING MY SPIRITUAL GIFTS

Opening Prayer (1 minute)

Begin this session with prayer. Either offer the prayer yourself or invite a group member to pray. (Be sure to check with a person in advance before asking that person to lead the group in prayer. Let people know that you will not ask them to lead in prayer without advance notice.)

Preview (1 minute)

Introduce the goals of this session by reviewing the Preview section in the student book and explaining briefly what you'll be doing together in this session.

Bible Discovery (25-30 minutes)

Read the paragraph that introduces this section. Explain that the gifts you'll be reviewing in this session are the ones identified in Romans 12, Ephesians 4, and a few other passages.

Go over each gift definition quickly while reminding class members that all the gifts are treated more thoroughly in Part C: Gift Studies of the student book. Encourage people to make use of those studies throughout the course, especially the ones on their own particular gifts.

Take about two minutes with each gift.

- Read the Scripture portion that refers to the gift.

- Expand on "the basic idea" of the gift in a couple of sentences using ideas from the Gift Studies section (Part C) of the student book.

- Invite the group to comment on people they know (or know of) who have this gift.

Option: Instead of guiding the whole group through all the gifts listed in the student book, you could divide the gifts and passages among small groups of three or four persons; then have the groups report.

Personal Sharing (10-12 minutes)

Divide the class into small groups of three or four persons to discuss the share questions in this section. Invite general comments or questions before moving on to the next part of the lesson.

This would be a good time to comment on gift mixes. A gift mix is a person's combination of gifts. A person's gift mix is often more influential than a single gift in determining a person's ministry direction. (See question 7 of the FAQs About Spiritual Gifts [Part B, section 2] in the student book for more information.)

What's Distinctive About Spiritual Gifts? (10 minutes)

Use the content of questions 9-12 of the FAQs About Spiritual Gifts (Part B, section 2) in the student book to develop your presentation on the four questions for this part of the session.

Inform participants that their skills and talents will also shape their ministries. Pay particular attention to the distinction between spiritual gifts and ministry roles, and observe that the Gift Studies in Part C of the student book provide important teaching about the roles of gifts as a responsibility of all Christians. Give class members time to add comments or ask questions.

Pg 57-58

9 • **How do spiritual gifts differ from natural talents?** → *Specifically for building up the church and Advancing the kingdom of God.*

10 • **How are spiritual gifts different from the fruit of the Spirit (Galatians 5:22-23)?**

11 • **How do spiritual gifts relate to offices in the church?**

12 • **How do spiritual gifts relate to ministry roles?**

Encourage everyone to read the detailed answers to these questions in the FAQs section (Part B) of the student book.

Looking Ahead (1-2 minutes)

Build anticipation for your group's experience of completing the Discover Your Gifts Survey at home after this session. Show your group where the survey is found (after session 2) in their books, and mention that they can also do the survey online (see the survey instructions). Let everyone know that it will take about 30-45 minutes to complete the survey.

Note also that everyone should be prepared to share results from the survey at the beginning of the next session. You may want to invite the class to take a quick look at the section "What Are My Spiritual Gifts?" in Session 3 so that they know what to expect for participating.

If you haven't already done so recently, you as leader should complete the Discover Your Gifts Survey too.

Closing (4 minutes)

Close by leading the class in an expanded version of the suggested closing prayer ideas. Or ask people to return to their small groups and use the prayer ideas as an outline for a closing prayer time together.

CONFIRMING MY SPIRITUAL GIFTS

Opening Prayer (1 minute)

Ask two or three persons in advance if they will contribute to opening prayers. These do not need to be long. They should, if possible, reflect what the class has been learning about God and about spiritual gifts.

Preview (1 minute)

Use the Preview section to introduce the goals of this session to your group.

What Are My Spiritual Gifts? (15 minutes)

Tip: If you want another 10 minutes or so for this important activity, you can skip the Natural and Supernatural section and spend less time with the section How to Confirm Your Spiritual Gifts (in that case, make sure everyone focuses mainly on point 3, Analyze Yourself). Be sure to suggest also that everyone complete their unfinished exercises at home.

Divide the class into groups of three of four persons to report to each other on their top gifts and to give each other additional comments on one of their gifts. Let everyone know that after about 8-10 minutes you'll be calling the groups back so that someone from each small group can report on the gifts of another person in their group.

For example, a reporter from a small group can say, "We learned that _____ has the gift of _____ and has used it to _____."

Give the class time to hear about other interesting things—feelings, surprises, questions—that came out in the small groups.

Option: Make a Pie Chart
(additional 5-10 minutes)

Tip: To make time for this option, you could shorten the Bible Discovery time and ask people to complete any unfinished Bible Discovery work at home.

Plan ahead to make a pie chart that shows the variety of gifts your class members have. Have each person from each small group report on at least one gift of another person in their group. As each person reports, ask how many others in the class had the same gift(s). Keep a record of these numbers. Turn these figures into a pie chart large enough to be a visual aid for the whole class to see next week.

Bible Discovery (15-20 minutes)

Begin this section by reading 1 Corinthians 12:7-10 for the class, and make a few comments from the following discussion about the gifts mentioned in that passage.

Notice first of all the phrase "the manifestation of the Spirit" in verse 7. From this phrase some people in the history of the church have developed the term "manifestational gifts." These are often described as gifts that have a very strong supernatural element—in other words, the power in them lies beyond the normal experience of most believers.

As we can imagine, there is debate and skepticism about some of these gifts—especially healing, miracles, and tongues. Some church leaders treat them as nonexistent, while others overemphasize them, imparting to them and to people who use them a status far above that of other gifts and other believers.

In this course, we want to make clear that these gifts are biblical and real and that we should closely follow biblical guidelines and examples to learn about their use for the kingdom of God. In other words, we should ask, *What does the Bible teach about these gifts, and how did people in the Bible use them?* In particular, as much as possible, we should be sure to ask, *How did Jesus use these gifts to the glory of God and for the kingdom of God?*

While there is mystery connected with every spiritual gift, some gifts may seem a lot more mysterious than others. Some may even seem spectacular. But we make a mistake if we dwell on some gifts more than others or treat some as more important than others.

The apostle Paul, who talks about these gifts in 1 Corinthians 12-14 and in other passages, makes clear in his descriptions of the body of Christ that no member is more or less important than others, especially when it comes to the gifts they have been given. All gifts are "the manifestation of the Spirit," and all are "given for the common good" (1 Cor. 12:7). If we use our gifts in ways that do not show love or support the upbuilding of the kingdom of God, we are as nothing and we gain nothing (1 Cor. 13:1-3).

Take time for questions or comments at this point, but avoid getting bogged down in the much-debated issue of whether certain gifts are still valid today. Some scholars believe that some of the gifts that operated in the New Testament church have ceased to exist. Most biblical interpreters, however, acknowledge their ongoing validity without insisting on their practice. The Bible does not give a decisive answer to all our questions about these gifts.

As you did in session 2, take about two minutes with each gift listed in the student book.

- Read the gift definition and the Scripture portion that refers to the gift.

- Expand on "the basic idea" of the gift in a couple of sentences using ideas from the Gift Studies section (Part C) of the student book.

- Invite your students to try to identify someone who has this gift, but don't worry if they can't. It seems the church of Rome (Rom. 12:4-8) didn't make much use of some of these gifts either.

Option: Again (as in session 2), instead of guiding the whole group through all the gifts listed in the student book, you could divide the gifts and passages among small groups of three or four persons; then have the groups report.

Natural and Supernatural (5 minutes)

Take a few minutes to reflect on gifts that seem mostly natural and others that seem mostly supernatural. Think together about the gifts and categories listed in this section in the student book, and then discuss the points made in the closing paragraphs there.

How to Confirm Your Spiritual Gifts

(10-12 minutes)

Lead your group through the main points of this section. Read, underscore, or amplify what is already in the student book. Here are some thoughts to share or activities to suggest. Mention that the first four points here can serve as an exercise during this group session and that the rest are suggestions for ongoing follow-up.

1. Understand your gifts.
Reinforce the importance of using the Gift Studies section (Part C) in the student book to explore the gifts people have discovered. Share about your own experience of doing in-depth studies of your gifts.

2. Accept the fact that you are gifted.
Give people the opportunity to say the words suggested, or something like it, to someone else in the class.

3. Analyze yourself.

Give group members a few minutes to share their thoughts on the analysis questions with one other person in the class.

4. Pray.

Remind your class that prayers of *thanksgiving, submission*, and *supplication* are important. Ask them which one of these prayer elements is hardest for them to pray and why. Everyone will have an opportunity to pray privately at the end of the class session (see Closing).

5. Seek confirmation from other Christians.

Invite a few persons to share confirming comments they have received about their spiritual gifts. Share your own experience of receiving a confirming comment. Group members will have opportunity in the next two sessions to share more about their spiritual gifts and receive confirmation.

6. Get involved in ministry.

The proof is in the doing. In Session 5 we'll focus on using our spiritual gifts in ministry.

7. Evaluate the results.

Though the Discover Your Gifts Survey is a helpful tool, you will only know for sure how much you are equipped with certain gifts by using them in ministry.

Looking Ahead (1-2 minutes)

Remind group members that a study of their top gifts in Part C: Gift Studies will prepare them for the "What I Have Learned . . ." section of session 4.

Also encourage everyone to look through section 3 of Part B: FAQs About Spiritual Gifts in the student book before the next session. Share a tidbit or two from these readings that will whet people's appetites for more.

Closing (4 minutes)

Announce an individual silent prayer time. If people had time to work on the prayer suggestion earlier in the session (see point 4 under "How to Confirm Your Spiritual Gifts"), remind them of that.

If you have a song leader or choir member in the group, or if you're comfortable doing this yourself, end this session by leading the group in the prayer song "Spirit of the Living God."

THE SPIRITUALLY GIFTED CHURCH

Opening Prayer (3-5 minutes)

Start with a prayer in which you mention topics to pray about and then group members pray silently for brief periods. An example follows:

- *Thank* God for the spiritual gifts he has given. (silence)

- *Confess* any failure to respond to the Holy Spirit and to use the gifts the Spirit has given for service. (silence)

- *Ask* the Spirit for wisdom and understanding during this session so that everyone may understand the Lord's will and ways. (silence)

- *Commit* to discover, develop, and use the gifts God has given. (silence)

Preview (1-2 minutes)

Try to convey your own excitement about the content of this session. As you read through the preview, help everyone to see that renewal and growth of the local church are greatly enhanced through the discovery and use of spiritual gifts.

What I Have Learned About My Gifts

(10-12 minutes)

Tip: If you want about five more minutes for this important activity, you can shorten Pulling Our Thoughts Together (see option in that section below).

Have participants get into groups of three of four persons for this sharing time. Urge people to give confirming feedback, if they can, about the spiritual gift each person reports on.

Pie Chart Option (additional 3-5 minutes)

Tip: To make time for this option, you could have people cover one or two fewer passages in each part of the Bible Discovery section, and ask them to complete any unfinished work at home.

If you created a visual pie chart based on the gifts cited in session 3, present that here. The chart will show the distribution of gifts among class members and hint at the gift diversity in your entire church. Invite class members to comment. Reflecting on gifts in the wider church will make for a helpful transition into the Bible Discovery section.

Bible Discovery (18-20 minutes)

Clarify the Bible Discovery assignment and help everyone get started. Unless the class is very small, it's probably best to divide into small groups of three or four (probably the same ones used in the preceding section). Join one of the small groups for this exercise. Mention that the whole group will be "Pulling . . . Thoughts Together" in the next part of this session.

Pulling Our Thoughts Together

(10 minutes)

Read the quote from Howard Snyder for the class. Lead the class as a large group through the questions in this section. Try to summarize people's responses at the end of this exercise.

Option: You could shorten this section by about five minutes, if you like, by discussing only questions 1 and 3 in the student book.

Working and Waiting Gifts (5 minutes)

Read the explanation in the student book to your whole group, or ask for a couple of volunteers to share the reading. Discuss together the difference between working and waiting gifts. Trying to identify waiting gifts is particularly important for new believers or others who have had little ministry experience. It may also help members who are already involved in ministry to turn a corner and begin a new ministry direction.

Ask everyone to turn with you to the Waiting Gifts Survey in Part D of the student book. Highlight anything in the introductory paragraphs that might help group members understand waiting gifts. One of the assignments after this session will be to complete the Waiting Gifts Survey.

Looking Ahead (1-2 minutes)

Note the importance of completing the Waiting Gifts Survey and being prepared to discuss one's waiting gifts in the next class session. (Point out the section "What Are My Waiting Gifts?" in session 5.)

Closing (3-4 minutes)

Focus the closing prayer on the church as the gifted body of Christ. Highlight the prayer suggestions, and remind class members to include these kinds of things in their regular prayers.

USING MY SPIRITUAL GIFTS FOR MINISTRY

Opening Prayer (2 minutes)

As you lead your group in opening prayer, keep in mind that this will be your last session together. Ask God's Spirit to empower each of the class members as they seek to use their gifts for building up the body of Christ and for spreading the benefits of God's kingdom throughout this world.

Preview (1 minute)

All of our thinking about spiritual gifts comes to a head in this session as we think about ministries that flow from our gifts and we consider the empowerment needed to exercise these gifts.

What Are My Waiting Gifts? (10 minutes)

Divide the class into groups of three of four for this sharing time. Remind everyone that although they each have only a few minutes to report on their waiting gifts, they should aim, where possible, to confirm each other in their discovery of waiting gifts.

If you have more time, give the whole class an opportunity to hear about one or more of the discoveries made by the small groups. Invite and respond to questions that people may have about waiting gifts.

Bible Discovery (10 minutes)

You can probably do this exercise with the whole group if it is not too large. If you have 15 or more people, though, you may want to divide into groups of four to five persons. Ask for volunteers to read

each of the passages. Ask the questions and affirm answers.

Note that the first passage (Acts 1:8) does not specifically refer to empowerment *for spiritual gifts.* It simply underscores that the Spirit's empowerment is necessary for all ministry. Try to summarize people's responses in a sentence or two.

Imagine

Wrap up this part of the session by helping group members brainstorm what life could be like in a gift-conscious, gift-mobilized community. This course has focused on helping participants *discover and use* their gifts. Give people a chance now to imagine not only how they would use their gifts to build up the body of Christ but also how *they* would benefit from being part of this body, surrounded by spiritually gifted people.

Ask them to imagine, for example, that they are in a church with one hundred members. A need arises in *their own* lives. Around them, ninety-nine people with a wide variety of spiritual gifts become aware of their need. People in that church know their spiritual gifts and are using them for ministry.

What's likely to happen? What will life be like in such a community? The members in need will be served! They will be lifted up in their time of need, built up as members of the body of Christ.

This is God's purpose for us—to be a ministering body in this broken world.

This exercise may be a "wow!" experience for at least some class members. Most of them have been thinking so much about discovering and using their own gifts to serve God and others that they haven't thought much about other gifted members serving them.

Gifts and Ministry Passions

(8-10 minutes)

Read or highlight parts of the paragraphs in this section of the student book. If you have time, supplement your comments with ideas from question 27 (about ministry passions) of the FAQs About Spiritual Gifts (Part B, section 5) in the student book. Give people a few minutes to work through the questions under "Finding Out My Ministry Passions" in their books. Then invite them to reflect on their responses and to factor in what they are learning as they shape an action plan in the next part of the session.

My Action Plan (15 minutes)

Give people about eight minutes to complete their personal action plans. (Explain that it's OK if they can't complete the whole plan in that amount of time; they can at least make a start and share what they've written.) Then divide people into small groups of three or four persons. Give them about five minutes to share highlights of their action plans with others in their small groups.

Then, if time allows, reconvene as a whole class and invite comments and contributions from the small groups about their action-plan discussions.

Looking Ahead (2 minutes)

Emphasize again the value of the FAQs About Spiritual Gifts (Part B) in the student book. Note especially the questions in section 5 there—great questions with which to wrap up this course.

Encourage everyone to fill out the Ready to Serve! form (in Part D of the student book) and get it back to you within a week. Clarify how and when your class members should do this. They might also want to be in touch with ministry leaders in the church or in the wider community who may be able to help them find a place to serve.

Offer class members whatever assistance you can give them. Challenge everyone to continue

developing their gifts and to become active in fruitful gift-based ministries. (See also the "Follow-Up" section below.)

Closing (5-10 minutes)

Close this final session with a commissioning of all participants to use the gifts God has given them for ministry. A sample commissioning litany follows right after session 5 in the student book. If you can, take time to make this a meaningful occasion of commitment and celebration. In some situations it might be appropriate to have group members pair up and offer commissioning prayers for each other.

Follow-Up

Once your group members have discovered their gifts and are ready to apply them in ministry, it's important to have a follow-up plan to help everyone find a ministry setting in which they can use one or more of their gifts. See Appendix A of this guide for ideas on setting up a Gift Leadership Team that can implement an effective follow-up plan. If you do not have a Gift Leadership Team in your church, you'll want to propose starting one, or at least put in place some or all of the following strategies:

- Each person completes a "Ready to Serve!" form (in Part D of the student book), and the church office or other administrator receives a copy for reference and for use in placing persons in ministries that fit their giftedness.

- The class meets again in one month to review members' progress in implementing their gifts.

- Pair each member of the class with a partner. Partners hold each other accountable—checking back with each other two weeks after completing the course, and then again periodically, to encourage each other to use their gifts in ministry.

Middle school

Liv D.
Tiff S. ———→ Pastor Chris
Sydney C. →
Preston
Kayla S.
Roth S.

Check w/
Phil on
communication
to students

APPENDIXES

FORM A GIFT LEADERSHIP TEAM

This *Discover Your Gifts* course can be used as a stimulating education class that will benefit all church members who want to know and use their spiritual gifts. It can be incorporated into the regular educational structures of the church and can fit naturally under the guidance of the educational ministry team.

The course can also be used to move the whole church toward becoming a gift-conscious, gift-mobilized spiritual community. If that is your intent, you may want to consider installing a Gift Leadership Team. This is a team mandated to facilitate the process of gift discovery and mobilization in your church. The team continues its work until the whole church is structured and engaged in a spiritual-gifts approach to ministry.

Staffing the Gift Leadership Team

Choose team members who . . .

- know their spiritual gifts.
- are familiar with the church and its policies.
- support the overall vision of the church and pastor(s).
- understand that the church is meant to be a ministering body.
- are committed to the process of gift discovery and mobilization.

This team will naturally be composed of a team leader and one or more gift course instructors; you'll also want to consider including persons with counseling, communication, and record-keeping skills. The team should also include at least one staff member of the church.

Leadership Team Responsibilities

The Gift Leadership Team should . . .

1. Make certain that the church embraces a vision of ministry that is based on gifts and their use for building up the body of Christ for effective service in God's kingdom. The church's primary leaders must establish and own this vision.

2. Assess the need for discovery, development, and deployment of spiritual gifts. Ask questions like the following:

   - What percentage of the congregation knows their spiritual gifts?
   - How many are actually involved in ministry?
   - Will current church structures facilitate gift-based ministry?
   - Will some current practices or attitudes need to be reshaped?

3. Develop a gift-discovery strategy. Plan for and promote the gift-discovery course, recruit for classes, support instructors, counsel those completing the classes, and help them find ministries that fit their spiritual gifts.

4. Identify people who can advise and assist in placing persons who complete the course. These may be ministry leaders or specially selected consultants who serve as

- *interpreters* who help gifted persons to understand and interpret the results of their gift class experience.

- *ambassadors* for the church who present the church's style of ministry, explain current ministries, and identify specific opportunities for ministry.

- *advocates* who represent gifted persons to ministry leaders and support those persons throughout the placement process.

5. Identify and describe the church's ministry positions and the gifts needed to fill them. Encourage ministry leaders to actively recruit gifted members to serve in the ministries they lead.

6. Follow up with persons who are placed in ministry and with the leaders of those ministries. The goal is to have an upbuilding use of gifts for the whole body. Offer support and direction, suggesting changes and other ministry options if necessary.

7. Analyze the church's structures and make sure they facilitate gift-based ministry. Recommend necessary changes to the church's leadership group.

8. Recommend or begin new ministries where none now exist in order to provide ministry opportunities for gifted members.

9. Create a record-keeping system that identifies the spiritual gifts of persons and ministry positions. A computer database will be useful for this.

10. Continue to support, encourage, and pray for instructors and course participants. Recommend that people take the Discover Your Gifts Survey again every 3-5 years to help them reassess their gift mix and ministry direction. The Spirit's work in them may show that they are ready to engage their waiting gifts or develop additional gifts to use in ministry.

OPTIONAL WAYS TO USE THIS COURSE

We recommend using all five sessions of this course (along with several homework assignments) to help participants gain a general understanding of spiritual gifts and how and why they are used positively in the church. The FAQs About Spiritual Gifts and the Gifts Studies sections (Parts B and C) in the student book provide additional background for further study.

However, depending on a variety of factors, such as

- the size of your church or group

- the amount of spiritual-gifts training that people have already had

- the availability of interested participants, who already have busy schedules

- the availability of leaders who can teach the class

and more, there are many ways to adapt this course for the benefit of everyone involved. Keeping in mind that the goal of spiritual gifts discovery and training is to build up and help equip the church so that it can serve God effectively in this world, you may find one or more of these options helpful:

- three-session *Discover Your Gifts* course

- two-session course

- one-session class (perhaps as part of a new members class)

- one-day intensive workshop

- overnight retreat workshops

- whole-church *Discover Your Gifts* emphasis

Three-Session *Discover Your Gifts* Course

If you choose to use parts of *Discover Your Gifts* for a three-session course, here's a way to structure your time:

First Session

- Use session 1: What the Bible Says About Spiritual Gifts

- Have participants complete the Discover Your Gifts Survey (online or in the student book) and have their results ready for your next session (see instructions provided with the survey). *Note:* Each participant will need a student book in order to do the survey. The online survey requires an access code supplied with the student book.

Second Session

- Use the following sections of sessions 2 and 3:
  —What Are My Gifts? (session 3)
  —What's Distinctive About Spiritual Gifts? (session 2)
  —Natural and Supernatural (session 3)
  —How to Confirm Your Spiritual Gifts (session 3)

- Assign the reading of relevant FAQs About Spiritual Gifts (Part B) in the student book.

- Encourage participants to study about their own gifts in Part C: Gift Studies in the student book.

Third Session

- Use the following sections of sessions 4 and 5:
  —Bible Discovery (session 4)
  —Pulling Our Thoughts Together (session 4)
  —Bible Discovery (session 5)
  —My Action Plan (session 5)
  —Close with a commissioning of all participants; use the Commissioning Litany (session 5), abbreviated, if necessary.

- Assign the reading of relevant FAQs About Spiritual Gifts (Part B) in the student book.

- Encourage participants to meet with church ministry leaders who can help direct them into a ministry.

Two-Session *Discover Your Gifts* Course

If you choose to use parts of *Discover Your Gifts* for a two-session class:

First Session

- Use session 1: What the Bible Says About Spiritual Gifts.

- Have participants complete the Discover Your Gifts Survey (online or in the student book) and have their results ready for your next session (see instructions provided with the survey). *Note:* Each participant will need a student book in order to do the survey. The online survey requires an access code supplied with the student book.

Second Session

- Use the following sections of sessions 3 and 5:
  —What Are My Gifts? (session 3)
  —How to Confirm Your Spiritual Gifts (session 3)
  —My Action Plan (session 5)

- To reinforce the concepts you have taught, assign the reading of relevant FAQs About Spiritual Gifts (Part B) in the student book.

- Reinforce what students have learned in one-on-one follow-up sessions in which you confirm their gifts and help them find ministry opportunities.

One-Session *Discover Your Gifts* Class

This option may work well as part of a new members class at your church.

- Use session 1: What the Bible Says About Spiritual Gifts.

- Have participants complete the Discover Your Gifts Survey (online or in the student book; see instructions provided with the survey). *Note:* Each participant will need a student book in order to do the survey. The online survey requires an access code supplied with the student book.

- To reinforce session 1, assign the reading of some basic FAQs About Spiritual Gifts (Part B, section 1) in the student book.

- Reinforce what students have discovered from the gifts survey in one-on-one follow-up sessions; make suggestions for using their gifts in ministry.

One-Day Intensive Workshop

Segment 1 (9:00-10:00 a.m.)

Opening Prayer and Warm-up Exercise (session 1) . . . . 5 minutes

Bible Discovery (session 1) . . . . 25 minutes

Pulling Our Thoughts Together (session 1) . . . . 10 minutes

Unpacking a Definition (session 1) . . . . 10 minutes

FAQs About Spiritual Gifts* (Part B, student book) . . . . <u>10 minutes</u>

    3. Why are spiritual gifts given?

    4. What are the benefits of knowing our spiritual gifts?

                                                         60 minutes

Morning Break (15 minutes)

Segment 2 (10:15 a.m.-12:00 noon)

Bible Discovery (session 2) . . . . 25 minutes

Bible Discovery (session 3) . . . . 15 minutes

Personal Sharing (session 2) . . . . 10 minutes

What's Distinctive About Spiritual Gifts? (session 2) . . . . 10 minutes

Discover Your Gifts Survey (student book;
    participants work individually) . . . . <u>45 minutes</u>

                                               1 hr., 45 minutes

Lunch Break (45 minutes)

Segment 3 (12:45-1:50 p.m.)

What Are My Spiritual Gifts? (session 3) . . . . 15 minutes

How to Confirm Your Spiritual Gifts (session 3) . . . . 12 minutes

FAQ About Spiritual Gifts* (Part B, student book) . . . . 8 minutes

    16. What hinders Christians from discovering their spiritual gifts?

Study two or three personal working gifts (Part C: Gifts Studies,
    student book; participants work individually) . . . . 20 minutes

What I Have Learned About My Gifts (session 4) . . . . <u>10 minutes</u>

                                                    65 minutes

Early Afternoon Break (10 minutes)

Segment 4 (2:00-2:45 p.m.)

Bible Discovery (session 4) . . . . 20 minutes

Pulling Our Thoughts Together (session 4) . . . . 10 minutes

FAQs About Spiritual Gifts* (Part B, student book) . . . . 10 minutes

    18. How will the church benefit from understanding spiritual gifts?

    19. What happens when a church ignores spiritual gifts?

Working and Waiting Gifts (session 4) . . . . <u>5 minutes</u>

                                                     45 minutes

Mid-afternoon Break (15 minutes)

Segment 5 (3:00-4:00 p.m.)

Bible Discovery (session 5) . . . . 10 minutes

Gifts and Ministry Passions (session 5) . . . . 10 minutes

My Action Plan (session 5) . . . . 15 minutes

FAQs About Spiritual Gifts* (Part B, student book) . . . . 10 minutes

    23. What are some intentional ways to develop my spiritual gifts?

    24. What can a spiritually gifted person do to find a ministry?

    25. How can a church help its members develop spiritual gifts?

Discuss a Follow-up Plan (end of session 5, leader's guide) . . . . 5 minutes

Commissioning (session 5) . . . . <u>10 minutes</u>

                                                     60 minutes

*You may wish to have class members read these FAQs in their student books, or you could prepare ahead of time to summarize the FAQs and ask if people have additional questions about these topics.

Overnight Retreat Workshops

These options are similar in content but less intensive than the preceding one-day workshop. The plans outlined here give everyone time for an overnight break. This may be especially helpful if your retreat includes travel. Feel free to adapt the timing of these options to suit your own arrangements.

These options also give participants more flexibility for completing the Discover Your Gifts Survey online, if they would like to do so.

Option 1: Evening Start through Next Afternoon

If your retreat begins in the evening, the following plan will give people an overnight break after completing the Discover Your Gifts survey.

- Segment 1—7:00-8:00 p.m.

- Segment 2—8:15-10:00 p.m. (participants break away at 9:15 to complete survey)

- Segment 3—9:30-10:35 a.m. (next morning)

- Segment 4—11:00-11:45 a.m.

- Segment 5—1:15-2:15 p.m.

Option 2: Morning Start through Next-Day Noon

- Segment 1—late morning: 10:30-11:30 a.m.

- Segment 2—1:00 p.m.-2:45 p.m. (participants break away at 2:00 to complete survey)

- Segment 3—3:10-4:15 p.m. (or in the evening: 7:00-8:05 p.m.)

- Segment 4—9:30 a.m.-10:15 a.m. (next morning)

- Segment 5—10:45-11:45 a.m.

Option 3: Afternoon Start through Next-Day Noon

- Segment 1—1:00 p.m.-2:00 p.m.

- Segment 2—2:15 p.m.-4:00 p.m. (participants break away at 3:15 to complete survey)

- Segment 3—7:00-8:05 p.m.

- Segment 4—9:30 a.m.-10:15 a.m. (next morning)

- Segment 5—10:45-11:45 a.m.

Whole-Church *Discover Your Gifts* Emphasis

If you want to involve your whole church in *Discover Your Gifts* at the same time, you may want to include gift-focused preaching in Sunday worship services.

1. Preach on the major gift passages in Scripture (see sermon outlines in Appendix C of this guide).

   - In your messages use much of the content that would ordinarily be learned in the Bible Discovery sections of Sessions 1, 2, 4, and 5.

   - Use insights from the FAQs About Spiritual Gifts (Part B) in the student book to amplify points in your messages.

   - Use insights from the main teaching segments of Sessions 1-5: Unpacking a Definition; What's Distinctive About Spiritual Gifts?; Natural and Supernatural; Working Gifts and Waiting Gifts; and so on.

2. Suggest a time for people to complete the Discover Your Gifts Survey, and have them turn in their results for follow-up. You may also wish to have people complete the Waiting Gifts Survey and other assessments cited on the Ready to Serve! form (in Part D of the student book).

3. Provide opportunity for your listeners, perhaps after a message or after a worship service, to engage in the kind of personal sharing found in these sections:

   - What Are My Spiritual Gifts? (session 3)

   - What I Have Learned About My Gifts (Session 4)

4. Gather responses from the gifts survey(s) and/or Ready to Serve! form and use your records for ministry placement and future mobilization.

SERMON OUTLINES ON SPIRITUAL GIFTS

This section contains five outlines for sermons on the Bible's main spiritual gifts passages. Each outline features a Scripture passage, suggested topic, and theme.

This material is offered as a resource to help you shape your own sermons; use approaches that will work best in your own ministry setting for applying these passages of Scripture. We assume that you will do your own exegesis, commentary study, Scripture cross-referencing, and additional reading in each case.

Permission is granted to adapt these sermon outlines for use in your local church.

You Are Gifted

1 Peter 4:10-11

Every Christian has spiritual gifts and is called to use them to the glory of God.

Introduction

Introduce the series.

Define *spiritual gifts.*

I. Receiving Spiritual Gifts (1 Pet. 4:10a)

A. Spiritual gifts are given by God.

B. Each member of the body receives spiritual gifts.

II. Employing Spiritual Gifts (1 Pet. 4:10b-11)

A. We are to employ gifts.

B. We are to employ gifts for one another.

C. We are to employ gifts as stewards of grace.

Develop the concept of stewardship.

Relate "grace" *(charis)* to "gifts" *(charismata).*

D. We are to employ all gifts for God's glory.

Give illustrations of how using gifts by God's power brings glory to God.

Conclusion

Describe the effects of an active gifts ministry in the church.

Challenge your listeners to acknowledge by faith that they have spiritual gifts.

Encourage everyone to thank God for giving gifts to the church.

Challenge people to use their gifts in ministry roles.

One Body, One Spirit, Many Gifts

1 Corinthians 12:1, 4-27

The church is the one body of Christ, and its members have many different spiritual gifts, each given by the one Spirit of God, who distributes them according to God's choosing.

Introduction

Want to learn about the church? Look at yourself in a full-length mirror. The Bible describes the church as a human body. Passages such as 1 Corinthians 12, Romans 12, and Ephesians 4 use this metaphor.

Observe the importance of knowing about gifts (1 Cor. 12:1).

I. Gifts Are Abilities for Service
(1 Cor. 12:4-6)

   A. Gifts defined

      charismata, diakonia, energeimata

   B. Gifts distinguished

     1. from natural talents

     2. from fruit (Gal. 5:22-23)

     3. from roles belonging to all Christians

     4. from offices of the church

II. Gifts Are Given by the Spirit for the Common Good (1 Cor. 12:7, 11)

   A. Each Christian has a manifestation *(phanerosis)* and an apportionment *(diairoun)*. See also 1 Corinthians 14:26-32, 36-38.

   B. Gifts are not for personal profit or self-glory but are for everyone's good.

   C. Gifts are always given for ministry.

   D. We are dependent on the Spirit.

     1. This eliminates pride and competition.

     2. This makes the body coordinated.

III. There Are Many Different Kinds of Gifts (1 Cor. 12:8-11)

    A. Nine gifts are mentioned in verses 8-11.

    B. Two additional gifts are mentioned in 1 Corinthians 12:28-29:

        1. the gift of service (helping others)

        2. the gift of administration (guidance)

    C. The Bible's gift lists are not necessarily complete.

IV. The Church Is the Body of Christ (1 Cor. 12:12-13, 27)

    A. Christ's body has many members.

    B. Believers are mutually the body of Christ.

    C. Believers are individually members of the body.

    D. Believers are baptized into one body by the Spirit. Study the meaning of baptism.

V. The Church Is Like a Human Body (1 Cor. 12:14-26)

    A. As a body consists of many members, so does the church (12:14).

    B. As the members of a body cannot dissociate from the body, neither can the members of the church (12:15-16).

    C. As one member of the body cannot be the whole, neither can one member dominate a church's life (12:17-19).

    D. As the body is one body with many parts, so is the church (12:20).

    E. As the members of the body cannot dispense with each other, neither can the members of the church (12:21-24a).

    F. As the members of the body care for one another, so it should be in the church (12:24b-26).

Conclusion

Call for unity—a unity marked not simply by the absence of division but by the presence of a positive, cooperative, harmonious spirit among all members.

Each Person Has a Place in the Body

Romans 12:3-8

Each member of the church should have a balanced view of his or her abilities and potential place in the body of Christ. Each member of the body ought to use his or her gifts fully, for the benefit of the whole.

Introduction

An extended metaphor: A boy whose father owns an auto repair shop dreams he is in the shop one night. He hears the parts of a disassembled car arguing about which is most important, and which parts get the prominent positions. The parts settle their differences by each agreeing to do what each does best. In the reassembled car, each part ends up where it was intended to be, doing what it was made to do. All agree, finally, that this is the best arrangement.

I. Each Member Should Estimate Abilities Correctly (Rom. 12:3)

A. We ought to make a reasonable estimate of our abilities and not cherish exaggerated ideas of ourselves.

B. We ought to judge ourselves according to the amount of faith God has given.

II. Each Member Should Discover a Place to Serve in the Body (Rom. 12:4-5)

A. We have many members.

B. We have different functions. Because of this, we are dependent on one another.

C. We are one body in union with Christ.

D. We belong to each other and need each other.

III. Each Member of the Church Has Different Gifts (Rom. 12:6a)

A. Each member has received gifts. Every member is important to the function of the whole body.

B. The gifts of each member differ. Show the wisdom of this arrangement.

C. The source of spiritual gifts is God's grace. Gifts are an unmerited blessing.

IV. Each Member Is Encouraged to Use Gifts to the Fullest (Rom. 12:6b-8)

Describe the various gifts and their full use.

Conclusion

Do you see yourself as God sees you?

Do you know how important you are in the body?

Stress both the need to be committed to using one's gifts and the need to develop those gifts.

Sermon 4

Gifts for Building Up the Body

Ephesians 4:7-14

God provides gifted leaders to equip his people to minister to and build up one another.

Introduction

Like a dentist without instruments, a Christian without gifts is helpless. But a dentist needs more than tools. Training is also necessary. Similarly, a Christian needs both gifts and training in the use of gifts. God has provided gifted leaders to equip saints for ministry.

I. The Giver of the Gifted Leaders (Eph. 4:7-10)

A. Christ gives grace in great measure (John 14:12-13; Phil. 2:9; 1 Cor. 12:5; Rom. 12:3, 6). Relate Christ's giving of grace to the spiritual gifts.

B. Christ ascended "higher than all the heavens" (Eph. 4:10; see John 14:12c, 18; Acts 1:6-11). Show that the ascended Christ has not left us alone.

C. Christ fills all things (Eph. 1:23; Gal. 2:20).
The gifted, ministering church displays Christ's fullness.

II. The Roles of Gifted Leaders (Eph. 4:11)

A. apostles

B. prophets

C. evangelists

D. pastors and teachers

III. The Task of Gifted Leaders (Eph. 4:12)

A. To equip Christ's people for the work of ministry

B. To equip Christ's people for building up the body

IV. The Goal of Gifted Leaders (Eph. 4:13-14)

A. Unity of faith and knowledge
Show how unity results if gifts function well.

B. Christlike maturity
This is not a personal maturity but a corporate maturity (see Eph. 1:22-23).

C. Adult stability
Show how gifted leaders help make the faith of God's people secure.

Conclusion

Are you a gifted leader? Seek to equip others who are in ministry.

Are you a gifted believer? Become equipped; do the work of ministry; build up the body of Christ.

Sermon 5

Using Gifts with Love

1 Corinthians 13:1-3

Gifts are important, but love is more so.

Introduction

Emphasize the importance of spiritual gifts.
Indicate that love is more important, and tell why.
Define the love *(agape)* Paul is talking about.

I.   The Gift of Tongues Without Love (1 Cor. 13:1)

A. What is the gift of tongues?
Explain why Paul deals first with tongues.

B. The gift without love
Comment on the Corinthian abuse.

C. The gift with love
See 1 Corinthians 14:2, 4, 13, 22.

II. The Gifts of Prophecy, Wisdom, Knowledge, or Faith Without Love (1 Cor. 13:2)

A. Explain these gifts briefly.

B. These gifts without love

C. These gifts with love
Describe some helpful, love-exemplifying ministries that flow from the gifts.

III. The Gift of Giving Without Love (1 Cor. 13:3)

A. What is giving? Why is martyrdom mentioned in some Bible translations?
Martyrdom is a total giving of oneself.

B. Giving without love
Comment on dutiful giving.

C. Giving with love, and love-motivated willingness to serve and even die for Christ

Conclusion

Comment on the following:

*   parenting without love

*   other ministries, such as serving as church school teachers, elders, deacons, and so on, without love

Emphasize that God is the source of *agape* love. We need God's love in order to love selflessly.

BIBLIOGRAPHY

Calvin, John. *New Testament Commentaries: The First Epistle of Paul to the Corinthians.* Translated by John W. Fraser. Edited by David W. Torrance and Thomas F. Torrance. Grand Rapids, Mich.: Eerdmans, 1960, 1989.

Clifton, Donald O. and Marcus Buckingham. *Now, Discover Your Strengths.* New York: Free Press, 2001.

_____ , Albert L. Winseman, and Curt Liesveld. *Living Your Strengths.* Second edition. New York: Gallup Press, 2004.

Green, Michael. *I Believe in the Holy Spirit.* Grand Rapids, Mich.: Eerdmans, 2004.

Harrison, Everett F., Geoffrey W. Bromiley, and Carl F.H. Henry, eds. *Baker's Dictionary of Theology.* Grand Rapids, Mich.: Baker Book House, 1960.

O'Connor, Elizabeth. *Eighth Day of Creation: Discover Your Gifts.* Revised edition. Washington, D.C.: Potter's House, 2007.

Snyder, Howard A. *The Community of the King.* Downers Grove, Ill.: InterVarsity Press, 2004.

_____ . *The Problem of Wineskins: Church Structure in a Technological Age.* Downers Grove, Ill.: InterVarsity Press, 1975.

_____ . *Radical Renewal: The Problem of Wineskins Today.* Revised edition. Eugene, Ore.: Wipf and Stock Publishers, 2005.

Wagner, C. Peter. *Your Spiritual Gifts Can Help Your Church Grow.* Ventura, Calif.: Regal Books, 2005.